Grandpa Cliff's Verses

Clifford Leary

Outskirts Press, Inc.
Denver, Colorado

Outskirts Press, Inc.
http://www.outskirtspress.com

ISBN: 978-1-4327-3449-7

Outskirts Press and the "OP" logo are trademarks belonging to Outskirts Press, Inc.

PRINTED IN THE UNITED STATES OF AMERICA

Dedication

Rita Leary, my wife, who provides constant support
to my writing effort.

Sophie Leary, my mother, who at the age of 97 still
provides verbal pats on my head.

Donna Ellis, my daughter, who provided excellent
assistance in preliminary editing.

The Day They Let the River Down

The word was heard o'er hill and dale.
T'was enough to make most folks pale.
The dam at the mill needed much repair,
but high water wouldn't let the workers there.

An urgent problem, they all say.
It must be fixed and right away.
The experts discussed it round and round,
but no solution could be found.

Then at last, they all agreed
they would have to do a terrible deed.
There would be uproar in the town,
but they would have to let the river down.

"Save the fish," became the cry.
"Don't let the little creatures die."
The town's folks had harsh things to say,
thinking there must be another way.

A date was set and plans begun
to let the mighty river run.
Du Bay Dam was closed up tight
to hold the flow both day and night.

Despite complaints, no tears were shed
as the old Wisconsin rolled from her bed.
What a sight it was to see
jumping fish, stumps, and debris.

Slowly, slowly the water flowed
as more and more of the bottom showed.
The stream narrowed more and more
till one could walk from shore to shore.

People came from miles around
to view the sight of the muddy ground.
They came by motorcycle, car, and truck
to gawk at the black and smelly muck.

Traffic directors were stationed around,
directing those who were river bound.
All were eager and wanted to see
a sight they thought could never be.

Some walked in the slippery mud,
poking through the dirty crud,
hoping to find some hidden jewel
buried within a shallow pool.

Up the river along Highway 10
was a crew of hastily working men.
They netted fish from captive pools,
placing them back with their mainstream schools.

Questions were heard along the shore.
"Will the fish be gone forevermore?"
"Will the river ever be the same
after this shock to the entire terrain?"

And that was the story in our hometown
the day they let the river down.

St. Patrick's at the Holiday Inn

The celebration was planned very well,
but who would come no one could tell.
An Irish band came from afar
and green beer flowed free at the hotel bar.

Annette decided the girls should go.
They all agreed and took Lou in tow.
As they arrived the band played a tune with pep,
as clog-dancing lassies kept right in step.

It took just a moment or two
when a very handsome admiral came into view.
He remembered Mary from her days of yore.
They proceeded to dance around the floor.

A good-looking usher from St. Stanislaus
started talking to Betty and made her blush.
The band played a waltz and then they had a dance,
and you should have seen those two prance.

The superintendent from Emerson School
saw Gen and started to drool.
He rushed to her, bowed, and took her hand,
and they strutted their stuff to the Irish band.

One of the Nelson boys grabbed Jane by the hand
and started to step in tune with the band.
They both agreed that this was fun,
and kept stepping it off 'til the tune was done.

A Polish lad from the north side
looked about, and it was Debby he spied.
He asked her to come away from the door
and coaxed her out onto the floor.

Lou decided to try a green beer
so he took a seat at the bar.
Pretty girls all flocked around,
coming from near and far.

The band played on in that big hall,
and a great time was had by all.
Everyone there claimed Irish ancestry
but of course that really couldn't be.

A couple of fishermen stopped at the bar;
their names were Bill and Ken.
They planned to have a beer or two
and head on home again.

They drank and watched the dancers gliding by,
when all of a sudden a couple caught Bill's eye.
It was Debby and a young lad who held her tight.
Blood pressure soared as anger roared and Bill was
ready to fight.

It was just a moment or two when Ken saw Jane
come into view.
As he watched her dancing with the guy, his blood
started boiling too.
They put their beer glasses down and rushed out on
the floor.
They each grabbed a guy and shoved him toward
the door.

As women screamed, the fight was on—
a real Irish brawl.
Some of the lads had been itching for a fight,
not wanting to dance at all.

The scrape went on 'til the fighters had all had
enough.
With blackened eyes or bloodied nose, they had
shown their real stuff.
"Fightin' is more fun than dancin'" is what some
lads will say.
And they always like to practice on each St.
Paddy's day.

Rita and Cliff showed up following the fray.
They had missed the fun but assured Annette
they would arrive on time
next St. Patrick's day.

Jimmy J's

"They had a big party at Jimmy J's" is what a feller
said.
He was there and at one point, he thought they'd all
be dead.

The Riley boys were having a fight,
And that, they say, was a bloody sight.

Jim had George pinned to the floor
when Big John Brown came barging through the
door.

He was carrying a case that looked like a gun.
Everybody in the room wanted to run.

Big John took off his wide black hat.
He kicked off his boots and his chew went splat!

It looked like the place was going to riot,
with fightin' and shootin', then all turned quiet.

John opened his case and what do you know,
he pulled out a fiddle and he pulled out a bow.

Everybody gasped and looked around
as Big John's fiddle made a wonderful sound.

Somebody shoved the tables to the wall,
and dancin' began to fill the hall.

Nancy-O' yelled "Do-see-Do" as she grabbed the
nearest guy.
Mary- E' laughed with glee as she yelled, "Just
watch me fly."

Lynda hopped up on the bar and sang for everyone.
You could hear her from afar; boy, did they have
fun.

Donna skipped across the room
and did a fancy jig with an old straw broom.

Big John fiddled as everyone giggled; what a time
was had by all.
Folks will never forget the fun they had at Jimmy
J's, pub and hall.

Pretty Girls

All the girls walk down my street.
Boys, I tell you, what a treat.
Some are short and some are tall,
but fellows, you would like them all.

Some look chubby, some look thin.
All depends on the clothes they're in.
Some are smiling, some look sad.
None of them look really bad.

Some are blonds and some are red.
Some were black, now grey instead.
Any color can look sweet
when they come strutting down my street.

Come on, lads, come sit with me.
Sit on my porch, the view is free,
and it's bound to charge
your battery.

Growing Older

As I sit here in my easy chair pondering my life,
and think about my blessings, my thoughts turn to
my wife.
The years we've had together have been such a joy.
She's just the kind of lovely friend I've thought of
since I was a boy.

We both show signs of passing years,
some of gladness, some of tears,
but by and large, we've weathered well,
at least as far as I can tell.

We both have silver in our hair;
though a sign of age, we do not care.
A line or two shows on our face,
but really that is no disgrace.

Our figures have shifted over the years,
but not enough to give us tears.
Age takes its toll as we all know,
but it matters not 'cause I love her so.

Bean Soup

With a mighty wind
and terrific roar,
the hinges flew
right off the door.

The roof rose up,
then settled back,
but the garage door
flew right off the track.

The stench was terrible
to behold,
somewhat like sauerkraut,
thirty days old,

With just a tinge
of birdcage Poop.
Now, Rita, Please—
no more of that darn Bean Soup!!!!!

The Flivver

We headed for the dance
in that old flivver of mine.
I asked her to be my Valentine.

As we rounded the bend
toward old Blaine Hall,
it was evident the flivver
was going to stall.

I pumped on the gas
and adjusted the spark,
but with a mind of its own,
it decided to park.

With a beautiful moon
in the sky up above,
I thought we might spoon
and maybe make love.

I shoved the seat back
and edged over her way.
She was somewhat alarmed
and had sharp words to say.

"Get this flivver started,
and I do mean now,"
and just about then
her fist hit my brow.

Her swing caused the flivver
to rock to and fro,
and to both our astonishment
it started to go!

I grabbed for the wheel
and we were on our way.
I left the romancing
for another day. . .

Old Love

Smiling and laughing is my forte',
I'm bubbling over with love.
It is just so much fun this way.
Happiness fits me like a glove.

My husband is such a joy.
He brightens every day.
I knew him when he was a boy,
before I went away.

When I returned from way out west,
and settled back here at home,
I found that I still loved him best,
and now I'll never roam.

Meesha's Adventure

Meesha is a little fox with bushy tail and fur of red,
with pointy ears on the top of her head.
She is as pretty as can be;
she is a "movies" fox, you see.

Working out in the cold on a field of snow,
to her trainer she was told to go.
Out of her box and on the run,
Meesha decided to have some fun.

She grabbed a fake chicken
in her jaws,
and then there was
a moment's pause.

Then, up the hill
through the field of snow,
we were all amazed
as we watched her go.

Over the hill and up the road,
into the woods she ran.
First to the south, then to the north,
then back to the south again.

With fear in our hearts and radio in hand,
we spread out far and wide.
Trying to guess as best we could
where little Meesha might hide.

She was sighted once or twice
but then was gone again.
"She will never survive out here in the wild,"
said several of the men.

The farmer's wife was heard to say,
"The woods are full of fox.
If Meesha finds a friend out there,
she'll never return to her box."

This being mating season
gave cause to speculate,
Would Meesha stay out in the wild
if she found a loving mate?

One lady saw some tracks so large,
she thought for sure they were bear.
Frightened in the woods she was
and got right out of there.

The search was on in those north woods,
but time was passing fast.
No sign of Meesha could be found.
Must we give up at last?

Determined but with trembling voice I heard her
trainer say,
"We'll just keep looking and we'll find that little
rascal pet.
I've worked with animals many years
and never lost one yet."

Then came a lad with a little dog
who said that he would try
to track that fox through those deep woods
and find the wayward little guy.

With dog on leash
with sniffing nose,
it's off into the woods
he goes.

It was not long we heard him say,
"Hurry, bring the box.
There is something just ahead
looks mighty like a fox."

By the grace of God
and a small beagle hound,
tho late in the day
little Meesha was found.

There were shouts of joy
throughout the camp
when Dave returned
with the little scamp.

St. Paddy's Day

St. Patrick's Day is coming soon,
and on the radio,
they're playin' sad old Irish tunes
from many years ago.

The telly shows the pictures
of how it was back then,
and don't you know the sadness
makes me cry all o'er again.

My old Irish Granny, sittin'
in her rockin' chair,
told of all the hardship
they all endured back there.

They were starvin' by the thousands,
tho their hearts were pure and good.
The English lords had plenty,
still they came and took their food.

The sadness of it all
brings me tears this very day,
and the Irish hates the English
and 'twill be no other way.

Some day I'm sure
you'll have a chance
to visit the Old Sod,
and when you do you'll understand
her sons are blessed by God.

They cleared patches of the stony ground
so they could work the land.
But how they scratched a living there,
I ne'r will understand.

With stones so thick and grass so thin,
they had a lot of heart
to try and raise a crop therein,
or even want to start.

With all their courage and their work,
and tho they did their best,
the Famine took the upper hand
and many traveled west.

So here we are, transplanted souls.
Now America is where we roam.
But way down deep within our souls, dwells
a little bit of home.

Happy St. Paddy's to you!

Never Hire a Fiddler

Grandma Alice by the window,
in the high-back rocking chair,
providing bits of wisdom
with her own Irish flair.

We sat around and listened
in the dimly lighted place,
as the flickering flame of a kerosene lamp
lighted up her face.

Stories of Old Ireland
she brought up from the past,
through fact and fable, happy and sad,
our attention she held fast.

Her Irish eyes would sparkle,
in tellin' of the strife,
of English lords who were dealt their due
with musket, club, and knife.

And then she'd turn the stories
to the do's and don'ts of life,
from how to tell ripe melons
to how to pick a wife.

And one thing I remember,
still clear to me today:
"NEVER HIRE A FIDDLER,
ALL HE WANTS TO DO IS PLAY."

He'd rather play than plow the sod,
or plant the seed or pick the cob.
The music's in his soul, you see.
His one true love won't set him free.

So remember that, me laddies—
if there's hard work to be done,
shy away from fiddlers;
they're just for having fun.

The Farm

Oh, this old farm, which we hold dear,
we grew from babes to adults here.

Oh, the stories it could tell.
Many of them we know well—

Some of laughter, some of tears,
as we look back the many years.

Happy St. Patrick's

St. Paddy's Day will be here soon.
Let's all meet at Casey's saloon.
Point Special beer will be flowing free.
Of that you can be sure, by gee.

Everyone is Irish on Paddy's Day,
and that's the way it is, they say.
It's a day for wearin' of the green,
and that will be most plainly seen.

Those who hail from Kilarney
will be known by their tales and their blarney.
Those who come from Tralee
are known for their fightin', you'll see.

When we mix the fightin', the blarney, and beer,
there will be a great time of good cheer.
Riley will throw beer in bottles and all,
and glass will be flyin' off old Casey's wall.

O'Donnel and Mikels will square off in a huff
just to decide which one of em's tough.
O this I predict, just mind what I say,
as I was down at Casey's last St. Patrick's Day.

Pig Man Is Gone

Big rough Dan, a mighty man,
raised pigs as big and rough as he.
His wife was scrawny thin and tan,
mild and pretty as could be.

He beat her proper every day.
There wasn't much that she could say.
She cried and cried with lots of tears,
and this went on for many years.

He was nasty as could be.
A dirty rotten man was he.
He tended to his sows and boar
with little thought of anything more.

If she asked for any little thing,
he would box her ears until they'd ring.
Without regard he'd slap her face.
It was a terrible disgrace.

One day when things were really tough,
she decided enough was enough.
She took the gun with rifle bore
and opened wide the kitchen door.

As Dan was opening the pigpen gate,
she pulled the trigger, shooting straight.
Dan hit the ground in a pool of blood.
The only sound was one big *thud*.

That giant boar turned on his heel.
He decided Dan was his next meal.
On seeing this, the sows came too,
devouring Dan like he was stew.

Soon there was nothing left in that pigpen
to show where big Dan had been.
If someone called to see the man,
his wife would sweetly say,

"Sorry, Daniel is not here today."

Rufus Brown

Rufus Brown lived just out of town
in a grove of cottonwood trees.
He walked around with a great big frown,
and his pants had holes in the knees.

Rufus had a mule that he treated so bad,
it would make a strong man cry.
He fed the mule old moldy hay;
it's a wonder the mule didn't die.

He had a cow which was tied to a stake
or sometimes to a tree.
It got its water from a lake
when Rufus let her free.

His beagle hound was skinny too,
with table scraps to eat.
He was sometimes fed just an old shoe,
as if that were a treat.

Rufus was a mean old man,
as everybody knew.
When he came to town the children ran,
and his friends were very few.

A Day in Time

Daylight savings time has come this season.
And why? For what good reason?
Dark and cold comes the new day.
Whose idea was this anyway?

It's cold and snow is piled high,
and more is falling from the sky.
"It's just to fool ourselves," they say.
I wish we'd kept it the old way.

The doggone clock is an hour ahead,
but indicates I should get out of bed.
The whole idea is sort of hazy.
To reason it out would drive you crazy.

My mood is not the best this morn.
By all the bad things I am torn.
I monitor my blood pressure as I should,
and I find it is not good.

Losing sleep is just not fun.
But I must get up and run.
If the sun would only shine,
I'd probably feel just fine.

I might be just a bit constipated,
which makes me somewhat agitated.
But who can feel up to par
with things going on like the Iraq war.

How many more young boys must die
and join their comrades where they lie?
When will this damn war end,
and let us start a peaceful trend?

Why can't Jews and Arabs agree
to stop their religious killing spree?
The ancient arguments they hold
just don't make sense, as I am told.

In Africa they are dying too.
Does it make sense or just voodoo?
Columbia and Venezuela are making a nasty noise.
What is going on with those bad boys?

Here at home we hear the blare
of naughty politics everywhere.
Will Hillary or Obama get the golden ring?
Will the Democrats or Republicans then be king?

Good folks are losing homes everywhere.
This is bad news, I declare.
Gas prices are going through the sky.
The cost of living is way too high.

The earnings on my savings account
are so little they don't really count.
The interest on my CD's at the bank
is down so low it's in the tank.

With prices up and earnings down,
it causes a happy man to frown.

Recession is here, there is no doubt,
and what can a fellow do but pout.

And so, my dear, one thing is true.
The one bright spot in the day is you.
Just to make you aware of this,
I'd like to give you a little kiss.

Last Call

The juke box played so loud and clear,
yet was not heard 'cept by those quite near.
The smoky room was filled with boys,
and they were making lots of noise.

Laughs and cheers and mugs of beers,
and shouts & touts among the peers.
Great fun— Oh yeah, most would say,
with aching heads come light of day.

Buck banged his mug on the bar with glee.
"Barkeep, filler up for me,"
though he'd had his fill,
'twas plain to see.

Finally came the time of night,
when barkeeps boom with all their might—
"Last call."

When Burley Bill gave out the yell,
it was down the hatch & back to the well.
Everyone wanted one more for the road
before heading back to their abode.

Though it was hard for him to see,
Buck said, "Make that a double for me."
He gulped it down and headed for the door,
as Burley yelled, "There ain't no more."

The night was damp and dark and cold.
His truck started hard, as it was old.
Finally it caught & gave out a roar,
as he hit the gas & slammed the door.

Down through the valley & on up the hill.
Top speed it was, gave Buck a thrill.
Then up to the bend Buck didn't quite see,
and over the rail at full speed went he.

Shattering glass and twisting steel,
hurtled down the ravine with Buck at the wheel.
Then finally the crash against an old oak tree,
As Buck murmured softly, "Please, God, help me."

Then he heard the voice come through the wood,
and in his pain it sounded good.
It seemed far— yet very near—
very soft— yet very clear—
"Last call."

Snow

I just wanted you to know
how beautiful it is with snow.
To be so blessed as you can see,
why— it's almost ecstasy.
You may have your desert
and your rain.
It just gets wet,
then dry again.

But here at home, as you can see,
snow adds beauty to a tree.
So cry your heart out, little dear,
at what you miss,
not being here.

Ice Fishing

Ice fishing was the talk of the day
The big ones were biting in Emily Bay.

The lake was covered with a foot of snow;
the wind was strong with a northwest blow.

The sun hung low in the eastern sky,
the early morning moon still high.

Cracking heard sharply as we drove onto the ice.
We knew if it broke we'd pay a big price.

But onward and onward we slowly crept,
to reach where we thought the big fish slept.

There was Eddie & me and Bob and Nate,
the ice auger, sled, and a bucket of bait.

The auger would bark and growl and kick,
as it burrowed through ice more than two-feet thick.

Our voices echoed across the lake,
as we discussed the spot that each would take.

We drilled the holes, then lowered the bait.
Now we would have to sit and wait.

Over an open fire at the edge of the lake,
the coffee pot hung on an iron stake.

Sandwiches toasted over smoky fire
filled up our bellies to our heart's desire.

A big hollow trunk from a fallen tree
made wonderful seats for the boys and me.

We waited and watched the tip-ups offshore,
as stories were told of the days of yore.

Some were true and some were not,
but most of them made us laugh a lot.

Suddenly a flag went up.
Eddie jumped and dropped his cup!

He raced to the hole as the line rolled out.
A fish took his bait—there was no doubt.

We all ran out to watch the fun,
as the fish and the bait continued to run.

He took it out about thirty feet,
then stopped to swallow his morning treat.

"Give him time," we told Eddie.
"Tighten the line, pulling slow but steady."

Eddie waited as he knew he should,
then tightened up the line as gentle as he could.

Eddie knew he had a big fish on,
the way it tugged, swimming hither and yon.

Slowly but surely it was drawn near the hole.
He was headed straight up but then gave a roll.

As he passed by the hole we all noted his size,
and looked at each other as we gasped in surprise.

That fish was a lunker, so big to behold,
the size of which great stories are told.

Eddie tightened the line once more,
bringing his catch close to the fore.

Again and again, he brought the fish 'round,
nearer and nearer the hole to be found.

We watched Eddie work with sweat on his brow,
expecting he'd win the battle anytime now.

Slowly and carefully Ed worked the line.
We all agreed he was doing just fine.

He was just about to attain his goal,
but saw that fish was too big for the hole!

"Run for the gaff hook and do it with vigor;
run get the chisel, we'll make the hole bigger."

Eddie let the big fish run out,
as excitement and action was all about.

The ice chisel was worked with many a blow,
as the giant fish swam slowly below.

Chipping and chopping done hurriedly with care,
hoping the fish would still be there.

Finally a much larger hole was in sight,
and we peered down the hole with great delight!

That monster fish was still in view,
and the question now, just what to do.

Although Eddie was only twelve years old,
he was quite strong and very bold.

He tightened the line a little bit
as the big fish tugged the end of it.

Ed brought the line in, pulling slow and steady,
while the other three watched with the gaff hook
ready.

The fish came along, into the hole came his head,
and then a surprise that fishermen dread.

With a splash of his tail and dark look in his eye,
that fish spat the bait right out toward the sky.

Down toward the bottom he swam with great speed.
as the four stunned fishermen gasped at the deed.

At the very same time to the astonishment of all,
the bait dropped back and they watched it fall.

That tantalized fish, still hungry as before,
then angrily after the bait he tore.

This time he got hooked in a very firm way,
so Eddie pulled him in and saved the day.

Now the story is told for miles around
how little Eddie caught a fish weighing twenty-five
pound.

Soft Petaled Rose

I gaze and gaze with eyes ablaze
and wonder what your meaning be,
Soft Petaled Rose,

Surrounded by some Baby's Breath
as delicate as thee.
Your color goes from white to red to violet
of great intensity. Oh soft petaled rose,
is there more than I can see?

Does it mean love?
Does it mean like?
Or are you just a tease— soft petaled rose.

God alone could fashion a beauty such as thee,
and wonderment of wonders,
you end up here with me— soft petaled rose.

I'd like to hold the hand that got,
the hand that brought yon petaled rose to me.
But for the moment, your silent beauty
must keep me company.

Pick-Me-Up Bouquet

What?— What did you say—?

For *me*—?

A pick-me-up bouquet.

How can that be?

Flowers—

To brighten my day,

you say?

Just because it's dark and gray?

Wow—

Who but you— dear tender,

loving soul, would think of me—

and bring my spirits up

where they should be?

Mean Boss

That son-of-a-gun keeps us on the run
from morning until night.
He gets my cork so doggone much,
I almost want to fight.

He yells and hollers like he is mad,
as if we had done something bad.
We all work hard most every day,
and I tell you it's for lousy pay.

I am really at a loss
to see how he became the boss.
He is dumber than a rock;
I think he came from darn poor stock.

I'd like to wring his dirty neck,
but then I'd lose my job by heck.
There'll come a day, I tell you,
this rotten guy will get his due.

First A.D.

Little Billy is his name.
Movie sets are his domain.
From San Francisco, I am told.
He handles the set crew brave and bold.

"Quiet— please!"

"All right, folks,
two minutes to go.
We're going to make a picture show."

"Quiet now! Please!"
"*ROLLING*"
"*ACTION!!*"

So quiet now,
there's nothing heard.
Not even breathing of the bird.

"CUT!"

"Please move that stuff
to camera right.
I want to keep it
out of sight."

"QUIET PLEASE!"
"*THANK YOU.*"

"*AWNNK AWNNK*"

What was that sound
made through his nose yet quite profound?
It is quite different, so it seems,
*yet everyone knows that it means— **QUIET!***

"We are almost ready
to shoot again.
Where oh where
are the set dress men?"

"Two more minutes
to start this stint.
Let's see if we can
make a print."

"Now put all that food away.
We're working animals here today.
If a cookie is seen by one of these crows,
it's one black flash and away it goes."

"Quiet please!!"
"Rolling—
ACTION!!"

"That's a ***wraaaap!!!***"
"Thank you all
for a job well done.
Take a hike.
Go have some fun."

(under his breath)
"Got that done
just in time.

Thirty seconds
before overtime!"

And so it goes
day in and out;
sometimes smile
and sometimes shout.

Always busy,
on the go;
barely time
to say hello.

He knows his job,
and does it well,
and the entire group
thinks he is **swell**!!!

Campaign Blues

My eyes are blurry, my ears are sore.
I do not want to hear any more.
This campaign has gone on far too long.
It's just more of the same tired song.

The issues are lost and have turned to mud.
Both sides are calling now for blood.
We are forced to listen to story after story
as they bore us with their oratory.

The blues are up and the reds are down.
Both sides are vying for the crown.
Who will win we do not know.
I just wish they would shorten this awful show.

The Seasons

Oh, the wonder of it all—
first comes spring then summer then fall.
Amazing treats each in its way
bring joy to us, both night and day.

Spring brings new life to plants and trees
and a taste of the coming soft summer breeze.
Tulips, crocus, and daffodils
bring beauty to valleys, plains, and hills.

Lo the summer and all of its joys,
with baseball and swimming and girls meeting
boys.
Those warm summer nights with stars up above
with the smell of the lilacs, there is so much to love.

Some call it autumn, some call it fall,
but this is the season we love best of all.
The trees show their brilliance, the air is so pure,
the flowers in full color and we know they're
mature.

Old devil winter with the cold and the snow
follows the autumn, and this we all know.
With a blanket of white to cover the earth,
old Santa comes calling with laughter and mirth.

Bucking Black

About ten years old and back on the farm.
I tried many things that could have brought harm.
Riding the horses was always great fun,
but there were times it couldn't be done.

That black colt was a year old now
and time to break him in for riding or the plow.
I took him outside and tied him to a post.
He could travel ten feet at most.

This colt stallion's spirits were high
and he was a pretty big guy.
He had never been harnessed and never seen a saddle.
I knew it was possible I might have a battle.

I talked to him gently and patted his shoulder.
I talked and patted and I got a little bolder.
I managed to get a bridle on which he didn't like a bit.
He backed away and stomped 'til I thought he'd
throw a fit.

I stepped up onto the barnyard gate.
Aha, sez I, this will be great.
From here I'll hop right onto this colt
and hang on tight if he tries to bolt.

With one quick leap I was aboard,
and with a violent buck, he tossed me forward.
I had thought I was going to go for a ride
but instead ended up with very hurt pride.

Poetry Lesson: Write a Sonnet

Do I love you every day?	a
Will you be mine,	b
my valentine?	b
I love you more than I can say.	a
You keep my heart in disarray,	a
fluttering and quivering all the time,	b
until I am feeling so sublime.	b
Please say yes, to thee I pray.	a
Your answer, my dear lady love,	c
coming from your loving heart,	d
will be a message from above.	c
With this our real life will start.	d
As time goes on, it is you I will adore,	e
and I will love you thus, for evermore.	e

Sweet Thoughts

Though I can see
your eyes of blue,
I cannot touch the hand of you.

Your soft-spoken words
I almost hear;
the lips that form them
are not here.

Your fragrance faint
before my face,
but you're not here
to give it grace.

These sensings only
in my mind,
etched there by someone
soft and kind.

It's many years
that I've seen pass,
yet youth returns
with you, my lass.

And so it is
I pine and yearn,
as I await
for your return.

This day will pass
as most days do,
amid silence and
sweet thoughts of you.

My Aunt Loretta

With sparkling eyes and pretty face,
She always seemed to walk with grace.
The world was brighter when she smiled,
as I remember as a child.

She worked as a teacher,
which brought her joy.
I well remember a lesson
taught one little boy.

Down on the farm
many years ago,
she camped in the "Forty"
for a week or so.

There was she and her husband
and children three,
with a green canvas tent
'neath a great oak tree.

On a Sunday aft
she'd invited the clan
to join in the fun,
as Irish folk can.

There was Earl & Violet
and their two boys.
There was Dad & Mom
and their little joys.

What comes back most clearly
and I remember the most,
was the lesson she taught me
at the marshmallow roast.

Marshmallows? It is probably
safe to say,
I had not tasted
till that very day.

The very first one
brought such great delight;
I longed for a hundred
with all of my might.

"Aunt Loretta," I asked.
"How many do we get?"
She gave me a smile;
I remember it yet.

"As many as you like,
take them right from this shelf,
<u>but never, never</u>
<u>make a **pig** of yourself</u>."

This lesson I learned,
and I'll never forget.
Taught to me gently
by my Aunt Lorett.

Christmas Greetings

Well— HO—HO—HO
What-do-ya know,
another year has passed, by Joe.
We are all busy, this I know,
as scampering about, we go.

We dash off here, we dash off there,
not taking time to say we care.
Christmas comes but once a year,
with special thoughts of those held dear.

Our loved ones are scattered,
some near, some far.
Regardless of distance,
how dear they all are.

Friends and relatives, one and all,
let's take this moment to recall
the joys & pleasures we have had,
the times shared, both good and bad.

It's time to ring the bell and tell
we love each other good and well.
As we gather together with joy and good cheer,
we wish you Merry Christmas,
and a Happy New Year.

Obesity

Calories, Fat, and Fiber.
Check out every can.
Also watch the sodium;
it's not good for any man.

The scale just keeps on climbing,
so what's a guy to do?
My pants don't fit me anymore;
isn't that a kettle of stew.

I once was such a skinny kid,
most folks laughed at me.
And now they laugh 'cause I'm fat;
not humorous for me.

Yes, old age is creeping up
and belly is creeping out.
And that's the way it is for me;
there isn't any doubt.

This dieting is a killer,
just roughage stuff, you know.
Those cookies, cake, and ice cream
have all got to go.

That chubby little doctor
says that I am obese.
I wish he would look in the mirror himself
and let me have some peace.

My wife says it's exercise
that will put me back in shape,
as she measures me around the waist
with her darned old sewing tape.

So it's miles and miles I travel
on the treadmill every day,
and eating next to nothing,
hoping fat will go away.

This painful trip will end some day;
I'm almost sure of that.
But in the meantime,
what a battle, with, the fat.

Poetry??

Sonnet, Sestina, Pantoum, Villanelle.
Our leader says we must learn them well.
She says this is poetry great and fine,
even though it does not rhyme.

What a surprise it is to a lad like me
to find it is truly poetry.
Does it tell us a story of life or love?
Does it bring revelation from above?

Some will say yes and some say no.
As for me, I just don't know...

Lynda says rhyming is not necessary,
just so the words are in the dictionary.

Gladys quotes poets of great renown,
such as old "Studs" Terkel in Chicago Town.

Jenny says the meaning is oh so grand,
even though I do not understand.

Marlene sees happiness everywhere.
If it rhymes or not, she does not care.

Joan keeps urging to look deep for the thought,
to understand clearly what the writer has wrought.

Millie is absent today;
I'd like to see what she has to say.

Sonnet, Sestina, Pantoum, Villanelle,
Will I ever understand them, it is hard to tell.

A poem should be a song minus tune,
and delight our senses like a sweet perfume.

It should lift up our hearts in a joyous way,
and for now, that's all I have to say!

Retired

When a feller sez to me
he'd really like to be
retired, 'stead of workin',

I tells him right out
he don't know what it's all about.
Jes' quit his complainin'
and keep on sustaining.

I sez to him
werkin' keeps ya in trim.
It keeps yer muscles firm
and yer belly thin.

Jes' keep on a werkin',
keep the brain just a perkin'.
Keep yer eye on the ball
and be a benefit to all.

You will also see
the time you have free
on a job that's to yer like-in.

There's holidays and weekends
for your fishin' and relaxation.
They seem so special
there's a lot of satisfaction.

Having every day off,
as great as it may seem,

should be nothing but pleasure,
but that's only a dream.

So keep on truckin' as long as yer able.
It makes ya feel important
and puts grub on the table.

Berry Picking

The sun is shining, the snow is melting.
Spring is here to stay.
It won't be long 'til the blossoms come,
then blueberries on the way.

The woods will be full of berry plants,
laden with berries of blue.
I will be picking berries with Rita,
my sweetheart oh so true.

We will pick a while
and rest a while in the forest green.
We will laugh a lot and hug a bit,
as long as we can't be seen.

When our buckets are full
we will head on home,
thinking thoughts of fresh baked pie.
A happy couple as we skip along,
under the azure sky.

She is ten and I am twelve;
our life has just begun.
And picking berries with Rita
is just the greatest fun.

As the years go by and we grow old,
and possibly part our ways,
we will always remember the fun we had
in our blueberry-picking days.

Rita

As days go by
I seem to see
that you become
more dear to me.

Where this will lead
we cannot say,
but just for now,
enjoy today.

We do not know
what lies ahead.
We place our trust
in God instead.

So fair of face
with tender heart,
I've really liked you
from the start.

To have a friend
as nice as you
is more than I'm
entitled to.

Fall

Four beautiful seasons every year—winter, spring,
summer, and fall.
If I must choose which I hold dear, the latter is the
best of all.

Winter with its snow and cold
comes on so nice but soon turns old.

I welcome spring when all turns new
and am happy to see summer too.

But real beauty do I see
as color adorns every tree.

October's days are a delight,
displaying clouds of whitest white.

The sturdy oak from green to brown;
the sumac red all over town.

The yellow maple all aglow;
I see it everywhere I go.

So fresh and crisp the morning air;
I see beauty everywhere.

Yes, autumn is the time I love;
for this I thank the Lord above.

Winter Blues

How long will this winter last?
So unlike those of recent past.
It alternates between snow and cold.
The pattern's getting mighty old.

I clear the drive all nice and clean,
then minutes later who is seen?
The big road plow comes round the bend
and fills the drive all up again.

I'm so darn tired of shovel and scraper.
This job belongs to a landscaper.
Tired and weary when job is done,
I hope this storm is the last one.

I dream of many warmer climes
where breezes are warm
and the sun always shines.
Then I wonder if I should go
and leave behind this pile of snow.

The Love of My Life

Though I have grown quite old and gray
and the spring has left my step,
my heart is full of love for one that's
always full of pep.

She smiles at me with eyes of blue,
so soft, so gentle, and so true.
Her heart is tender as can be—
a lovely lady, all can see.

Without her I would be alone
and lonesome as can be.
I thank you, Lord, for bringing her
so very close to me.

Leaves

October at our "ranchette"
is something to behold.

All colors of the rainbow, and more,
readily unfold.

The Apple, Oak & Maple,
Cherry, Aspen & Pine—

all aglow in color,
just beautifully divine.

Though Man with all his effort
may strive forevermore,

he'll not approach the beauty
God presents out our back door.

Slim, Sard & Chink

And so they were both brave and bold,
these eager lads of yore.
Adventure filled their hearts and minds,
as they headed west for more.

Primitive roads and sometimes trails
they followed on their way.
But westward, ever westward
a few miles every day.

The Model-T Ford chugged along
o'r valley, hill, and plain.
Through the mountains, over the desert,
and other rough terrain.

The land was relatively new;
so much, they had not seen.
From prairie wide to mountain high,
and oh the forest green.

With money short they worked their way,
picking at rock for gold.
The work was hard but they were tough,
these eager lads of old.

In apple orchards ripe with fruit,
they brought the harvest in;
and when that task was finished,
they traveled on again.

On to the sea and down the coast
to Californ-i-ay,
a traveler they befriended
caused them problems on the way.

He drove the Ford right off the road
and smashed her whole front end.
And when he saw the damage done,
he hightailed round the bend.

Myron came from Oakland
and took them back with him.
He found a house and then some work
for Sard, then Chink and Slim.

The winter went by quickly
and soon turned into spring.
The "call of home" was beckoning,
so they packed up again.

They sold Slim's car, drove Myron's truck,
and headed south and east.
From time to time their roadside meal
was a jackrabbit feast.

They made it to El Paso
and crossed the Rio Grande.
Their throats were parched from desert heat
and dusty blowing sand.

Mexican tequila
was the treatment, so they say.

It took a day of resting after, and
they continued on their way.

Up across Texas
and into Arkansas,
and the worst of muddy roads
any of them ever saw.

They would shove and push
until they couldn't anymore,
then stop and rest
'cause their muscles were so sore.

They headed north
toward Illinois.
By now, they were
very tired boys.

A few more days
and they found rest.
They made it home
from the trip out west.

Trip out West

They tour no more the mountain peaks,
nor visit sandy shore.
Their resting place not far from home,
these fine young lads of yore.

They've run the course
and left their mark
for all the world to see,
and now reside in God's own hands for all eternity.

We visit now the quiet spots,
where they've been laid to rest.
Our minds go back and again we say,
"Tell us about your trip out west."

Winter

Early in the morning, I pull the shade to see
new snow has covered everything from lawn to
bush to tree.
At least six inches of that stuff—
I wonder, is it wet or is it fluff?

If wet, the blower doesn't work and shovel it will
be.
At any rate, that man upstairs has made some work
for me.
My wife says, "Oh how beautiful," but I have other
views,
as I dig out my heavy coat and high-top winter
shoes.

I toil away while not yet day in early morning light.
At last, when done, the drive is clean and shovel out
of sight.
I go inside, hang up my coat, and put my wet boots
in a bin.
I hear a noise, look outside, and see a snowplow fill
that drive again.

The seasons here are wonderful and new snow is
nice, it's true,
but an hour on the shovel can change your point of
view.

Spring

I saw a robin yesterday high up in a tree.
All fluffed and hunkered down as he sat watching
me.
The air was cold and a breeze blew strong.
Robin knew winter was lasting much too long.

Today I saw a different sight: three robins in a row.
They pecked around in my backyard where soon
green grass will grow.
The ground's still froze so worms are few;
some other food will have to do.

Who knows what they will find to eat,
as they peck and scratch with their little feet.
Their red breasts glow in morning sun
as forth and back I see them run.

Spring is here at last when they return,
and summer breezes we all yearn.
Old man winter has had his day.
Now it's good to see him go away.

Wake Up!

Wake up! Wake up! you sleepyheads.

It's time to get out of your comfy beds.

The sun is high up in the sky.

The breeze is gentle and the air is dry.

This day is nice and all brand new,

and such great things await for you.

Your little dog couldn't wait anymore,

so he pooped a pile on the kitchen floor.

You smile and say, "Who cares, little dear.

It's just so nice to have you near."

The Weebs

Who are those gals who are sitting there,
at the far end of the Wooden Chair?
They seem to be having so much fun,
then all at once, they up and run.

Apparently it's to work they go
that makes them want to hurry so.
Retired they all seem to be,
so work can't be the urgency.

Relax at breakfast and some gab
is what these ladies really had.
Over many years it's been this way,
and does continue until this day.

It's Nancy, Rita, Betsy, and Dori,
all pretty ladies, it's plain to see.
They have named themselves appropriately.
<u>W</u>e <u>E</u>at <u>E</u>arly <u>B</u>reakfast for <u>S</u>anity.

Writing Class

Our writing class is such a joy.
The girls all smile, and so does Roy.
Jane is the one who leads the way,
asking, "Is your lesson done today?"

Marty leads off with mystery deep,
as at the edge of our chairs we keep.
Each chapter of her story's told,
about handsome lads she's known of old.

Alva, who once was a WAC
stationed near New Jersey's shore,
tells tales of many prisoners of war.
The German and Italian boys, though under guard,
were far
from home,
so kindhearted Alva let them roam.

Mildred is the technical one,
correcting our errors just for fun.
She writes for a statewide writing group,
so is privy to all the latest writing scoop.

Toni is planning to write about squirrels,
how they bury their nuts and why their tails have
curls.
Meanwhile she wrote about poor widow Brown,
whose spirits were raised by a trip downtown.

Roy missed class the last couple times.
He might have lost interest in our stories and
rhymes.
If he returns, Jane will lead a cheer,
"Welcome back, Roy, we are happy you are here."

School Is Out

Well, my friends, the time has come.
We gather up our books and run.
We tidy up all nice and neat;
our sessions here are now complete.

Minnie told us of her moth,
which flew off into the sky.
Was it really a moth?
Or was it a butterfly?

Toni's squirrel lives happily
in the top of an old oak tree.
This time next year, there will probably be
more baby squirrels to see.

Marty's long story will soon unfold,
with tales of riches in that black gold.
We hope her research finds that she
is the real beneficiary.

Mildred's story we have not yet heard,
but she is the master of the printed word.
She will soon be writing at high speed
a story I'm sure we'll all want to read.

Jane too will have to go;
we'll leave her with her high-school beau.
She has inspired us all to do our best,
and now it's up to us to do the rest.

So class is over one and all;
perhaps we can resume next fall.
It has been great meeting with all of you,
but for now, it's a fond adieu.

The Writer's Lament

My sheet is blank,

and, it appears, a writer I'll not be.

I try in vain to set down words;

just can't get in the mood, you see.

There are other things that I must do,

and so to you I say,

My time for rhyme is limited.

I'll write another day.

Printed in the United States
141792LV00002B/4/P